ENGLISH/ARABIC

# The T♥ddler's handb♥♥k

with over **100 Words** that every kid should know

BY DAYNA MARTIN

الإنجليزية / العربية

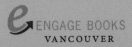
ENGAGE BOOKS

VANCOUVER

ENGAGE BOOKS

*Mailing address*
PO BOX 4608
Main Station Terminal
349 West Georgia Street
Vancouver, BC
Canada, V6B 4A1

www.engagebooks.ca

*Written & compiled by:* Dayna Martin
*Edited, designed & translated by:* A.R. Roumanis
*Proofread by:* Reem Mokhtar
*Photos supplied by:* Shutterstock
*Photo on page 47 by:* Faye Cornish

FIRST EDITION / FIRST PRINTING

LIBRARY AND ARCHIVES CANADA CATALOGUING IN PUBLICATION

Martin, Dayna, 1983–, author
    The toddler's handbook : numbers, colors, shapes, sizes, ABC animals,
opposites, and sounds, with over 100 words that every kid should know /
written by Dayna Martin ; edited by A.R. Roumanis.

Issued in print and electronic formats.
Text in English and Arabic.
ISBN 978-1-77226-448-7 (bound). –
ISBN 978-1-77226-449-4 (paperback). –
ISBN 978-1-77226-450-0 (pdf). –
ISBN 978-1-77226-451-7 (epub). –
ISBN 978-1-77226-452-4 (kindle)

1. Arabic language – Vocabulary – Juvenile literature.
2. Vocabulary – Juvenile literature.
3. Word recognition – Juvenile literature.
I. Martin, Dayna, 1983– . Toddler's handbook.
II. Martin, Dayna, 1983– . Toddler's handbook. Arabic.
III. Title.

PJ6166.M37 2017          J492.7'181          C2017-905762-6
                                             C2017-905763-4

الحروف الأبجدية
Alhuruf al' abjadia

4

**ABCs**

الأعداد
Al' aedad

11

**Numbers**

الألوان
Al'alwan

14

**Colors**

الأضداد
Al' addad

16

**Opposites**

الأشكال
Al'ashkal

22

**Shapes**

الأصوات
Al' aswat

24

**Sounds**

الأفعال
Al'afeal

28

**Actions**

العواطف
Aleawatif

30

**Emotions**

الرياضه
Alriyaduh

32

**Sports**

المحركات
Almuharikat

34

**Engines**

الأحجام
Al'ahjam

36

**Sizes**

الجسم
Aljism

38

**Body**

أدوات المائدة
'Adawat almayida

40

**Tableware**

الملابس
Almalabis

42

**Clothes**

وقت الاستحمام
Waqt alaistihmam

44

**Bath Time**

ميعاد النوم
Miyead alnuwm

**Bed Time** 45

3

# Aa

تمساح إستوائي
Tamsah 'iistwayiy

**Alligator**

دب
Daba

# Bb

4 **Bear**

قطة
Qata

# Cc

**Cat**

كلب

Kalb

# Dd

## Dog

فيل

Fil

# Ee

## Elephant

ثعلب

Thaelab

# Ff

## Fox

معزة

Mueiza

# Gg

## Goat

# Hh

حصان
Hisan

## Horse

# Ii

الإغوانا
Al' iighwana

## Iguana

# Jj

نمر
Namur

## Jaguar

6

الكوالة

Alkawala

Kk

**Koala**

أسد

'Asada

Ll

**Lion**

فأر

Far

Mm

**Mouse**

سلمندر

Slmndr

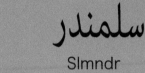

Nn

**Newt** 7

قندس
Qandus

# O o

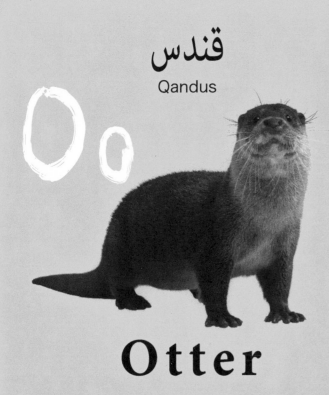

## Otter

خنزير
Khinzir

# P p

## Pig

السمان
Alsaman

# Q q

**8**  ## Quail

أرنب
'Arnab

# R r

## Rabbit

كلب البحر
Klb albahr

**S** s

**Seal**

نمر
Namur

**T** t

**Tiger**

سعدان الواكاري
Suedan alwakary

**U** u

**Uakari**

نسر
Nasir

**V** v

**Vulture  9**

ابن عرس
Abn eurs

# Ww

**Weasel**

سمكة
Samaka

# Xx

**X-ray fish**

ثور التبيت
Thawr altabiat

# Yy

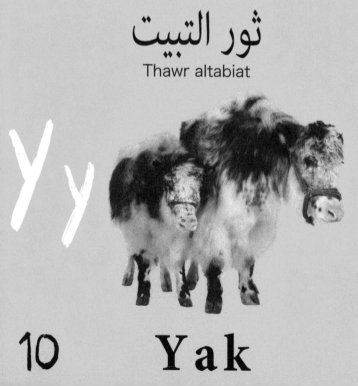

10

**Yak**

الحمار الوحشي
Alhimar alwahshiu

# Zz

**Zebra**

تفاحة

Tafaha

واحد

Wahed

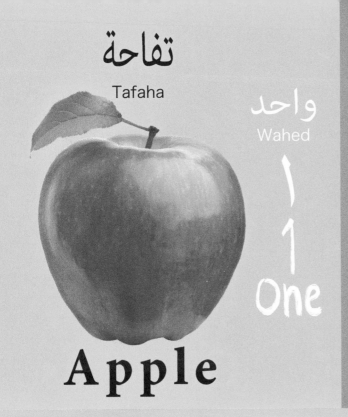

١

1

One

**Apple**

المقرمشات

Almuqarmashat

اثنين

Ethnein

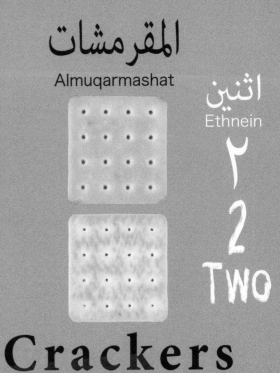

٢

2

TWO

**Crackers**

شرائح البطيخ

Sharayih albatikh

ثلاثة

Thalatha

٣

3

Three

**Watermelon slices**

فراولة
Farawila

أربعة
Arba-a

٤

4

Four

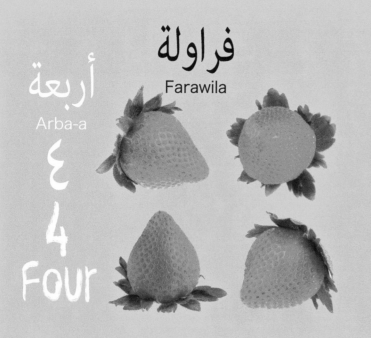

# Strawberries

جزر
Juzur

خمسة
Khamsa

٥

5

Five

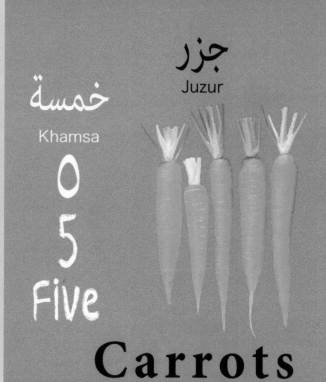

# Carrots

طماطم
Tamatim

ستة
Sitta

٦

6

Six

12

# Tomatoes

# قرع
## Qarae

سبعة
Sab-a

٧

7

Seven

## Pumpkins

# شرائح الفاكهة
## Sharayih alfakiha

ثمانية
Thamanya

٨

8

Eight

## Fruit slices

# بطاطس
## Batatis

تسعة
Tis-a

٩

9

Nine

## Potatoes

# بسكويت
## Baskuit

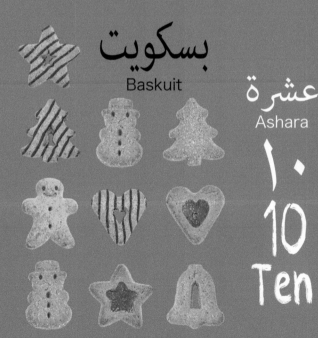

عشرة
Ashara

١٠

10

Ten

## Cookies

13

قوس قزح

Qus qazah

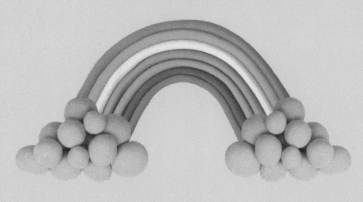

# Rainbow

أحمر

'Ahmar

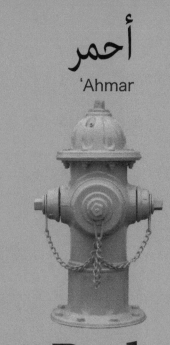

# Red

برتقالى

Birtaqalaa

# Orange

أصفر

'Asfar

# Yellow

أخضر
'Akhdir

# Green

أزرق
'Azraq

# Blue

اللون النيلي
Allawn alnayliu

# Indigo

بنفسجى
Binafsjaa

# Violet

15

فوق
Fawq

# Up

أسفل
'Asfal

# Down

داخل
Dakhil

# In

خارج
Kharij

# Out

16

ساخن
Sakhin

# Hot

بارد
Barid

# Cold

مبلل
Mubalal

# Wet

جاف
Jaf

# Dry

17

أمامَ

'Amam

**Front**

خلف

khalf

**Back**

يشعل

Yusheil

**On**

يطفىء

Yatfaa'

**Off**

18

مفتوح
Maftuh

**Open**

مغلق
Mughlaq

**Closed**

فارغ
Khashab

**Empty**

ممتلئ
Mumtali

**Full**

19

آمنة

Amina

# Safe

خطير

Khatir

# Dangerous

كبير

Sagheer

20 # Big

صغير

Kabeer

# Small

نائم

Nayim

**Asleep**

مستيقظ

Mustayqiz

**Awake**

طويل

Tawil

**Long**

قصير

Qasir

**Short**  21

دائرة
Dayira

# Circle

مربع
Murabae

# Square

مثلث
Muthalath

22 **Triangle**

مستطيل
Mustatil

# Rectangle

معين
Maein

# Diamond

نجمة
Najima

# Star

بيضوي
Baydwy

# Oval

قلب
Qalb

# Heart   23

## Sneeze

عطس
Eats

اتشووووو
Atashu wawawaw

Ah-choo

# Sneeze

## Duck

بطة
Bata

كواااك
Kawaaaak

Quack

# Duck

## Cow

بقرة
Baqara

مووووو
Muwuwaw

Moo

24 # Cow

## Phone

هاتف
Hatif

تررررن
Terrern

Ring

# Phone

قرد
Qarad

اووو اه
Awew ah

او و اه
aweww ah

Ooh-
ooh-
ahh-
ahh

**Monkey**

ضفدع
Dafadae

ريبيت
Ribit

*Ribbit*

**Frog**

اصمت
Asmat

شششش
Shshshsh

*Shh*

**Hush** 25

ديك
Dik

كوكو كو
Kwkw kw

Cock-a-
doodle-doo

## Rooster

طبول
Tabul

بوم بوم
Bum bum

Boom

## Drums

ثعبان
Thueban

Hiss

هسسسس
Hassss

26 ## Snake

بومة
Bawma

هوووت
Hawawut

Hoot

# Owl

نحلة طنانة
Hulat tinanatan

دزززز
Dazazaz

Buzz

# Bumblebee

يدين
Yudin

تصفيق
Tasfiq

Clap

# Two hands

حمل
Hamal

ماااااء
Maaaaaa'

Baa

# Lamb 27

يزحف
Yazahaf

## Crawl

يتدحرج
Yatadaharaj

## Roll

يسير
Yasir

## 28 Walk

يركض
Yarkud

## Run

يثب
Ythbu

**Hop**

يركب
Yarkab

**Ride**

يقبل
Yaqbal

**Kiss**

يقفز
Yaqfaz

**Jump** 29

سعيد
Saeid

# Happy

حزين
Hazin

# Sad

غاضب
Ghadib

30 # Angry

مذعور
Mazoor

# Scared

محبط
Muhbat

# Frustrated

متفاجئ
Mutafaji

# Surprised

مصدوم
Masdum

# Shocked

شجاع
Shujae

# Brave

31

البيسبول
Albaysbul

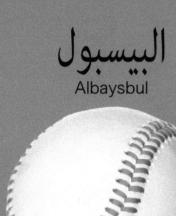

# Baseball

كرة السلة
Kurat alsala

# Basketball

التنس
Altanas

كرة القدم
Kurat alqadam

32 **Tennis**

# Soccer

تنس الريشة

Tans alraysha

**Badminton**

كرة القدم الأمريكية

Kurat alqadam al' amrikia

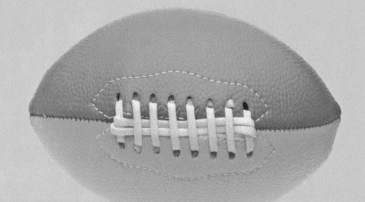

**Football**

الكرة الطائرة

Alkurat alttayira

**Volleyball**

جولف

Julif

**Golf** 33

سيارة إطفاء

Sayarat ʼiitfaʼ

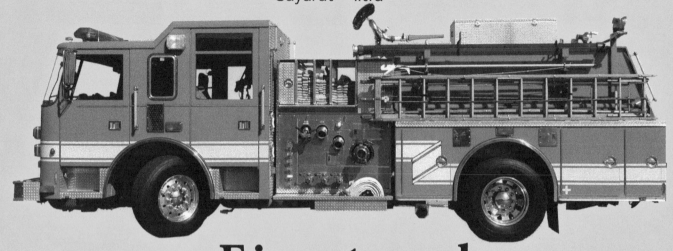

# Fire truck

سيارة

Sayara

**34** **Car**

شاحنة

Shahina

# Truck

هليكوبتر
Hilykubtr

# Helicopter

طيارة
Tiara

# Airplane

قطار
Qitar

# Train

قارب
Qarib

# Boat 35

صغير
Smôl

متوسط
Mtwst

كبير
Kabir

**Small** **Medium** **Large**

صغير
Smôl

متوسط
Mtwst

كبير
Kabir

**36 Small Medium Large**

كبير
Kabir

متوسط
Mtwst

صغير
Smٍl

**Large      Medium      Small**

كبير
Kabir

متوسط
Mtwst

صغير
Smٍl

**Large      Medium      Small      37**

رأس
Ras

# Head

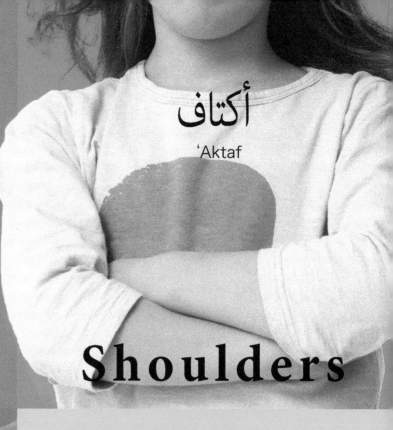

أكتاف
'Aktaf

# Shoulders

الركبتين
Alrukbatayn

# Knees

اصابع القدم
'Asabie alqadam

# Toes

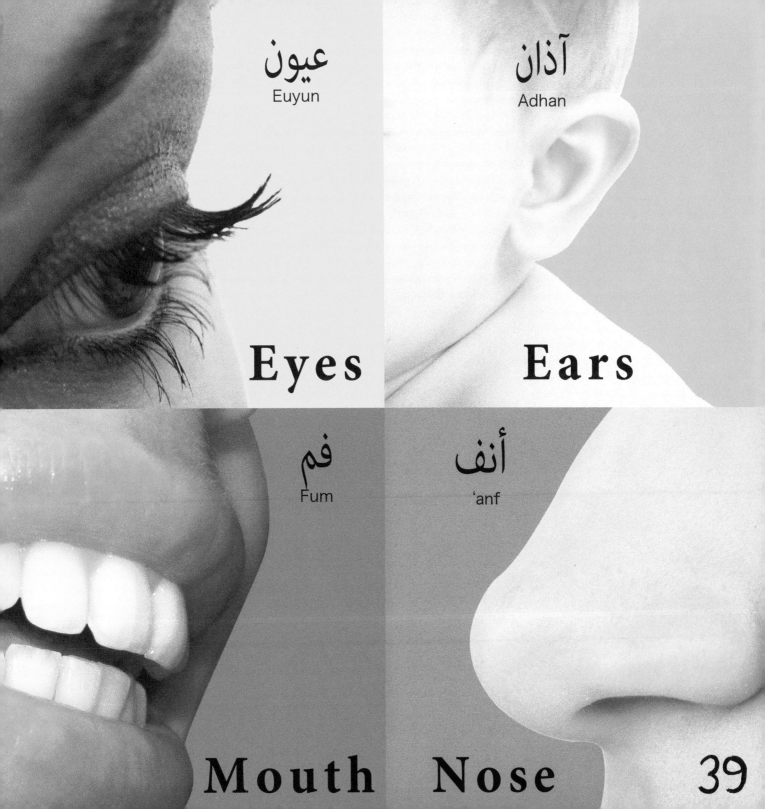

عيون
Euyun

**Eyes**

آذان
Adhan

**Ears**

فم
Fum

**Mouth**

أنف
'anf

**Nose**

39

كوب الرشف
Kub alrashf

# Sippy cup

وعاء
Wiea'

# Bowl

قدر
Qadar

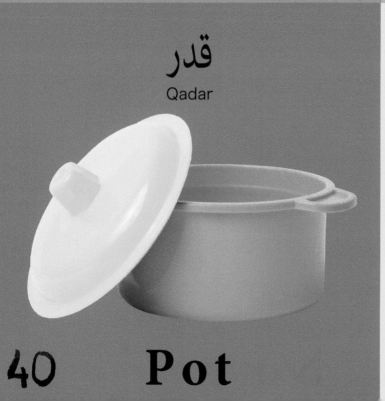

**40** **Pot**

كوب
Kub

# Cup

طبق
Tabaq

# Plate

شوكة
Shawka

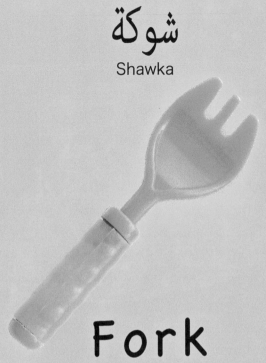

# Fork

سكين
Sakin

# Knife

ملعقة
Maleaqa

# Spoon

41

قبعة
Qabea

# Hat

قميص
Qamis

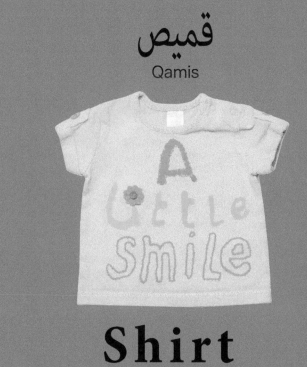

# Shirt

بنطال
Binital

42 # Pants

شورت
Shuirat

# Shorts

قفازات

Qafazat

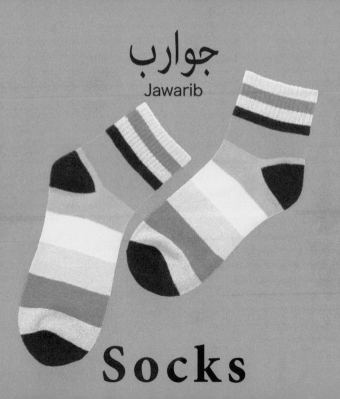

# Gloves

نظارة شمسية

Nizarat shamsia

# Sunglasses

جوارب

Jawarib

# Socks

أحذية

'Ahadhiya

# Shoes  43

وقت الاستحمام
Waqt alaistihmam

الاستحمام
Alaistihmam

Bath time

**Bath**

صابون
Sabun

بطة مطاطية
Butat mutatia

44 **Soap**

**Rubber duck**

أغسل أسنانك

'Aghsal 'asnanak

# Brush teeth

وقت النوم

Waqt alnuwm

*Bed time*

كتاب

Kitab

# Book

القصرية

Alqasria

# Potty

السرير

Alsarir

# Bed

45

# THE T♡ddler's handb♡♡k

activity / سؤال
Sual

Match the following to the pictures below.
Can you find **7 pumpkins**, an owl,
a rainbow, a baseball, a lion, a square,
a sad boy, a helicopter, and shoes?

وصل الكلمات الأتية بالصور: يقطين, بومة ,قوس قزح
,البيسبول, أسد,مربع, فتى حزين, هليكوبتر, أحذية؟

Tayirah hilikubtr
طائرة هليكوبتر
helicopter

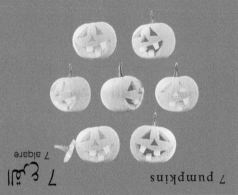

'Ahadhiya
أحذية
shoes

Albawma
البومة
owl

Albaysbul
البيسبول
baseball

7 alqare
7 يقطين
7 pumpkins

Fataan hazin
فتى حزين
sad boy

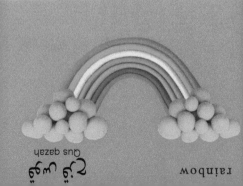

'Asada
اسد
lion

Murbae
مربع
square

Qus qazah
قوس قزح
rainbow

46